W9-DFU-151

FROM FROZEN NORTH TO FILTHY LUCRE

From Frozen North to Filthy Lucre

RONALD SEARLE

with remarks by
GROUCHO MARX
and commentaries by
JANE CLAPPERTON

A Studio Book · The Viking Press · New York

First published in 1964 by The Viking Press, Inc., 625 Madison Avenue, New York, N.Y. 10022
Published simultaneously in Canada by The Macmillan Company of Canada Limited
Library of Congress catalog card number: 64-23351. Printed in the U.S.A. by The Murray Printing Co.

AUTHORS' ACKNOWLEDGMENT
Without *Holiday* magazine and its art director, the incomparable Frank Zachary, there would have been no book; several outraged citizens from points between Alaska and Palm Beach would have been just as glad, but you can't please everybody. Most of these drawings, and part of the text, originally appeared in *Holiday*. All those concerned are deeply grateful for permission to reprint this material, parts of which are Copyright © 1961, 1962, 1963, 1964 by The Curtis Publishing Company.

CONTENTS

Foreword	9
Alaska	11
Canada	26
Provincetown	36
Wall Street	44
New York World's Fair	58
Tourist Washington	76
Tribal America	90
Florida	96

My knowledge of art is infinitesimal. I know that Rembrandt was deaf (no, that was Beethoven). I know that Van Gogh got hungry one day and cut off his own ear and that Toulouse-Lautrec walked around on his knees. And that's about it.

So for me to write an extended frontpiece for Ronald Searle's collection would not only kill the sale of the book, but would also ruin what is left of my vanishing career.

However, it does not need the curator of the Museum of Modern Art to tell the world that Mr. Searle is a genius. Whatever the price, the buyer will be getting all the best of it.

Groucho Marx

ANCHORAGE WESTWARD HOTEL
TAXI
Ronald Searle

FOREWORD

The glorious names of history's great travelers go ringing down the corridors of time—Marco Polo, Christopher Columbus, Stanley and Livingstone, and now Ronald Searle. For years Mr. Searle has been pottering neatly about the globe, disguised as the agent of an international spy ring and putting up a convincing pretense of sketching military installations, missile sites, the bathrooms of ambassadors, and similar classified areas. Since so many other people were simultaneously doing the same sort of thing, the CIA knew where it stood and nobody cared a rap. The time has now come to blow Mr. Searle's cover. What he was really up to all this time was drawing people, which, as everybody knows, is infinitely more dangerous.

What is currently setting the chancelleries of the world on their ear (an advanced yoga position helpful to constructive thought) is that the penetrating survey of North America anatomized in these pages is the work of foreigners, and English at that. The Anglo-American alliance, on which the sun never sets, may well be in peril. To set the record straight, and I think we ought to do this right away before the FBI men come with the big black car and take us away, this book is not a mean, malicious, Communist-inspired attack. It is an amused and affectionate report, a sort of fantasy on a theme by George Washington, drawn and written by two people who are as fond of America and Canada as anybody going and quite apt to get all choked up over maple leaves and star-spangled banners.

The only thing that remains to be said is that if you have half as much fun looking at this book as we had doing it, you will be off to the booby-hatch in no time at all.

—JANE CLAPPERTON

Alaska

Alaska was discovered in 1741 by a Dane called Vitus Bering who happened to be looking for it. Bering was in the pay of the Russians, which in those days was perfectly all right; Russians, as is well known, are very fond of fur, which they make into hats, coats, and lap robes for droshkies, and since the only other people around were so preoccupied with the question of whether to spell themselves Eskimos or *Esquimaux* that they never advanced beyond one set of sealskin underwear apiece, the visitors were able to help themselves to the surplus. By 1867, however, every muzhik's wife had three fur coats and enough is enough, so Alaska was sold to the United States for $7,200,000, or a little over $12 a square mile. Thirty years later a folk hero called Dangerous Dan McGrew tipped a pebble out of his mukluk, or chewed-reindeer-hide boot; it shone in the light of the midnight sun with an unearthly radiance, and in no time at all there was the Gold Rush, which led to a lot of uncultured goings-on but was a good thing on the whole, since gold is always useful.

There was also, of course, the Yukon, which had been there all along but suddenly began getting publicity, chiefly through the efforts of Robert W. Service. Mr. Service, though a master of the sounding phrase, would have been a problem to the Alaska Visitors Association, had there been one at the time; in his view the North was tough sledding and no place for weaklings, to whom he referred, with salutary bluntness, as scum. The march of civilization has changed all that, and since the territory's admission to statehood in 1959 it has been an everyday affair for even quite fragile people to go from one end of Alaska to the other without being so much as torn in pieces by a maddened dog team. The worst that can happen to a tourist in Alaska today is to have his credit card eaten by a bear; Mr. Service would find it all very tame.

Bargains in bears are offered by the bush pilots of Alaska,
who whisk the jolly hunter from ice floe to ice floe
in search of the bigger, better bear.
But, slice it where you like, transportation always comes expensive.

National
BANK
OF
ALASKA
ANCHORA
FUR RENDEZVOUS
515

Alaska clings to the old ways; a homesteader's cabin
is still his castle, and trappers still bring
their pelts (uninhabited, as a rule) to the trading post at Fort Yukon.

NC
TRADING
POST
FORT YUKON
Scalps
All colors

The blessings of civilization are mixed;
but even in Alaska
some people like to keep up with the times.

The Eskimos are a sturdy people, and whales are always welcome.
The inhabitants of Point Hope maintain that their village
has been a happy harpooning ground for several thousand years,
which goes to show that some whales never learn.

The people at Headquarters
will never believe a word of this.

Dumb friends all over the world are getting more sophisticated,
not to say tricky, with every passing day.
Probably there is nothing to be done about it.

The Alaska Highway runs through the state for only 306 of its 1527 miles, but the ride has natural hazards that are all its own.

Although new hotels and motels are popping up all over the tundra, there is still room for the one-man business.
(Real Eskimo ice cream is made from reindeer fat or seal oil whipped up with snow, and is not everybody's cup of tea.)

ALCAN HIGHWAY
DANGER
ANIMALS
CROSSING

This progress lark is an insidious business.
Not only has it seriously affected the takings of Klondike Kate,
but nobody can pretend that it's as much fun
panning for gold by the light of the silvery neon.

CHENA BAR
BAR
STAR LIQUOR STORE
THE DOG HOUSE
Cocktails
ELBOW ROOM
SAVOY BAR
BOTTLE SHOPPE LIQUOR STORE
Barbecue
COCKTAILS
ARCTIC LOANS
ELBOW
BAR
NUGGETS
GIFTS
Ronald Searle

The climate of Alaska is trying,
and bush pilots,
who are subject to special hazards,
rely on long underwear and little bits
of fur strapped to the kneecaps.
Though there are some very fancy
radar installations, space travel
has not yet come to Alaska;
or, on second thought, has it?

Canada

Canadian history got off to a somewhat leisurely start. Leif Ericson struck the coast a glancing blow round about the year 1000, but matters were hushed up until 1497, when Canada was discovered all over again, this time by Cabot. For the next thirty-seven years everybody milled around saying, "What shall we do about Canada?" except for the French, who chauvinistically favored the form, *"Qu'est-ce qu'il faut faire à l'égard du Canada, hein?"* Eventually, however, the situation firmed up, and several people went there (including Henry Hudson, who got lost). Then, in 1759, General Wolfe took Quebec, discontentedly remarking at the time that he would rather have written Gray's "Elegy." Since Gray had written it already there was nothing to be done about this, and four years later the whole country was turned over to the British.

Like so many parent-child relationships, Canada's ties with the mother country are tinged with ambivalence; while for the most part deeply, even tearfully, loyal to the Crown, the Canadians have a sensitive regard for their own identity, and anything that looks to them like condescension is poorly received. French Canadians are even touchier about France, and the attitude of both groups to those other people south of the border is characterized by a truly massive ambiguity. It is all rather difficult. Canadians, on the whole, know what they are not; but once the process of elimination has exhausted itself, perplexity sets in.

What, precisely, is a Canadian? The theory (long cherished by outsiders) that between the 49th parallel and the North Pole there is nothing much but Mounted Police, lumberjacks, and Paul Muni in a fur hat is clearly inadequate. Perhaps, if we wait a little while, the Canadians will decide for themselves who, and what, they are, and then let us into the secret; in the meantime, Ronald Searle's balefully entertaining impressions may be relied on to add to the confusion.

Ronald Searle
The Dew Line

Calgary has a Stampede; it has it in July,
and suddenly the sidewalks are littered with the bodies of those
who have just tripped over their spurs for the fourteenth time.
The other thing Calgary has is the chinook, a hot wind
which doesn't do a thing except melt snow.

The industrious habitant of the Ile d'Orleans has his own problems;
with a *bébé* under every *chou*, sometimes a man feels he just can't go on.

Victoria, in British Columbia, provides a trim, nostalgic haven for the Bath-chair brigade; it is kinder not to point out that the name of Her current Majesty is Elizabeth.

Things are not what they were in Henry Hudson's day.
But, though nowadays more than half of Canada's fur production is supplied
by farms, the solitary trapper scores when it comes to variety;
there's more in the woods than mutated mink.

In Port Radium, in the Northwest Territories,
the merry music of the Geiger is a bit muted these days.
The invention of overkill has had an adverse effect
on the uranium boom, since there is already enough of the stuff
above ground to blow up pretty nearly everybody.

Ronald Searle
Indian River
Vancouver

One of the reasons the Pilgrims took ship in the first place
was to get away from outmoded customs like eating fish on Friday.
The fact that they ended up on Cape Cod proves it is no good running away from things.

Provincetown

In 1620 the Pilgrims waded ashore at the far end of Cape Cod, catching the most awful colds as a result. Later they founded a settlement there which, since they had to call it something, they called Provincetown. (Not right away, mind you; these things take time.) They had absolutely no idea what they were getting into. Pilgrims as a whole were inclined to gloom, but even in their most apprehensive moments they cannot have envisaged the welter of beards, Bermudas, and stretch-pants-encased bottoms that adorns the Provincetown scene three centuries later.

The people that live here all year round (a sturdy bunch numbering around thirty-five hundred) are wonderfully tolerant of summer visitors, possible because *le tourisme* is not the town's sole source of income. Provincetown lived by fishing when the motorcars that crowd down-Cape every warm weekend were only a piece of freakish foolery that would never replace the horse; if Provincetown had to, it could do it again. This converts the tourists from a necessary evil into a hilarious diversion, and makes for good relations all round. Another local industry was inflicted by a Mr. Hawthorne, who set up the Cape Cod School of Art in 1899, thereby unleashing scores of workers all slapping paint onto canvas in an attempt to improve its appearance. (Current top man in the patron class is Walter Chrysler; the automobile industry is thus contributing two ways to Provincetown's prosperity, a state of affairs which ranks high on the list of unforeseen consequences of the internal-combustion engine.) Then there are the people who collect bits of driftwood and furbish them up and make them into lamps. And anyone on Commercial Street who is not a fisherman, a painter, a tourist, or a driftwood-furbisher is probably an oceanographer playing hookey from the Institute at Woods Hole. In doubtful cases, the matter can be settled by a simple test question: "What are the wild waves saying?" If he tells you, he's an oceanographer.

Surrounding this sociologist's sandbox is a landscape that is considerably more basic: dunes, beach grass, marshes, moors, ponds, and, on three sides, the old sea self-absorbed and full of fish. Thoreau, who never greatly cared for crowds, once pointed out that at this last lost end of New England "A man may stand . . . and put all America behind him." Naturally no red-blooded, two-car-family American would want to do anything of the silly sort; but it is nice to know that, should he ever want to, there is somewhere he still can.

POWDER
POWDE
POWDER
POWDER
POWDER
Ronald Searle

Provincetown is full of perils, some of them due
to sheer carelessness; and those shops on Commercial Street
will do anything to bring the customers in.
Next year this couple will go back to the Adirondacks.

Even in Provincetown painters are beset by critics
who may not know a lot about art but do know what they like.

Ronald Searle

The colorful *paseo*, or march of the summer boarders,
enlivens Provincetown from May to September.
The gentleman dragging his anchor
is not a fisherman but an escaped artist;
all the fishermen were up at four a.m., fishing,
and are now home trying to get some sleep.

The Dow-Jones Avera
MARKET DIARY
Ronald Searle

Wall Street

To some people Wall Street is a way of life, to others a symbol of bloated capitalist nastiness; it all depends on where you stand. For those fair-minded persons who like to see things for themselves, a good place to stand is on Manhattan Island between Trinity Church and the East River. Innocents who want to know where the Wall is are likely to end up having somebody sell it to them, along with the Brooklyn Bridge and Paul Revere's horse; but the Street is still there and, despite periodic fits of the vapors when some blabbermouth lets slip the word r*c*ssion, it is doing nicely thank you.

To look at, it is not imposing; the narrow, one-way street is only seven blocks long, and, though such monuments to the free-enterprise system as the House of Morgan and the New York Stock Exchange give off the appetizing smell of money, it is perfectly possible to walk the whole twilit length of Wall Street without knocking off a single top hat. As for being crushed by a falling financier—once a grave hazard—the chance is so remote that insurance companies no longer trouble to include it in their lists of the circumstances in which they will not pay out one bent nickel. This undramatic state of affairs is disappointing to the out-of-town visitor, but those who make a living in the district find it very restful. A man who has paid up to 200,000 dollars for the privilege of walking fifteen miles a day on the floor of the Stock Exchange (this punishing routine is what causes brokers to laugh bitterly when their occupation is described as "sedentary") is in no fit state to worry about anything much beyond Standard and Poor's Index and the frightful ache in his metatarsals.

There are seventeen million stockholders in the United States, and more than half of them are women. This somber thought haunts the hapless broker as he sits at eventide with his feet in a bucket, wistfully contemplating his new Matisse through the rising steam. Sooner or later women will crash the most sacred purlieus of the exchange; soprano giggles will profane the Stock Exchange Luncheon Club; female bullfighters and bear-leaders will take over the whole unpredictable menagerie; and what will then become of the old ideals of probity, integrity, and high seriousness? What indeed.

A smoking-hot tip is what everybody wants.
Financial-page reporters, whose dream it is to make their
readers rich, gather what crumbs they can without thought
of personal inconvenience; this makes them the only people
around Wall Street who are not counting the cost.

THE WALL STREET JOURNAL
NEW YORK STOCK EXCHANGE
THE UNITED STATES OF AMERICA
ONE DOLLAR
WALL
BROAD ST
NASSAU ST
ONE
DID YOU RISK a $25 FINE TODAY?
DONT LITTER
Ronald Searle
Wall Street

The New York Stock Exchange, proverbially fond of animals, houses three species of dumb friend. The bulls know which stocks will go up, the bears know which will go down, and the vultures take care of the bad guessers.

The paper industry is greatly indebted to the exchange, which discards a ton of the stuff every day. Much (though not all) of this consists of calculations hastily jotted by brokers who are too proud to add up on their fingers.

JCP 46½ PNC 14 ARV 1000S 33 TXN 95 5½
1030
26
New York Stock Exchange
Ronald Searle

If the muted, zoolike rumblings of the Stock Exchange Luncheon Club
are sifted with care, they are sometimes informative. Even
in this enclave of dark brown wealth, however,
Morgan seldom tells Merrill Lynch (let alone Pierce, Fenner, or Smith).

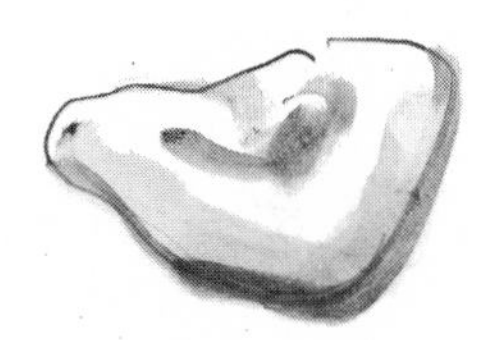

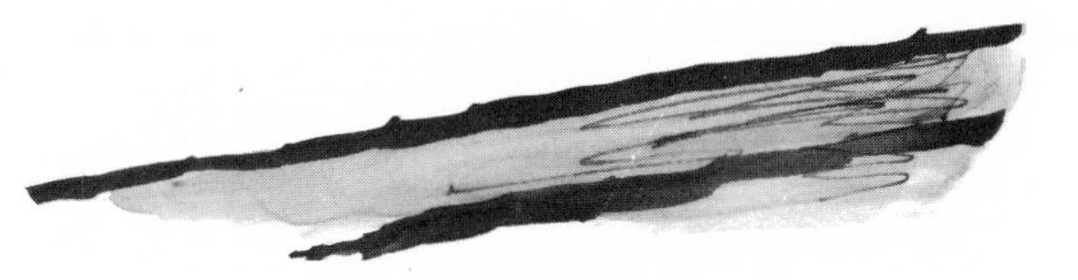

Some titans of the Street may be immune
to the prevailing passion for art,
but a nice bit of engraving is always appreciated.

Ronald Searle

One-stop shopping for groceries and government bonds is yet to come, and hardly any brokers give trading stamps.

Not all investors while away a wet Thursday afternoon by cornering wheat;
the distance from the piggy bank to American Tel. & Tel.
(or just plain T, as it is cozily known to the ticker tape) gets shorter every day.

Anyone who wants to get ahead on the Stock Exchange must learn to decode the Delphic chatterings of the ticker tape (the letter Q, for instance, stands for bankrupt companies). Even on a good day, about fifteen errors creep in; bad days do not bear thinking about.

Ronald Searle

MAMMON
WE SALUTE YOU
Ronald Searle

A Roman triumph for that popular figure, Mammon, is long overdue; as patron of the touchy market, he thrives on the smoke of burning dollar bills.

The Wall Street Journal belongs to the Dow-Jones Co., which also keeps an Average. Then there is the Dow Theory, a superior form of ESP which enables those who understand it to make a bundle. Oddly enough, most forms of gambling are illegal in New York.

For the Illinois Pavilion,
Walt Disney has built a life-size
Lincoln animated enough to scare
the daylights out of you.
It talks, sits, stands, gestures,
raises either or both eyebrows,
and would go streaking back to
its log cabin given half a chance.

New York World's Fair

There is a widespread notion that World's Fairs are planned as a glorious contribution to progress, prosperity, culture, scientific knowledge, and international chummery. This is of course nonsense. A World's Fair is occupational therapy in its gaudiest form. Cities, like people, go through phases when they feel restless and combative, unsure of their identities, and generally under-appreciated; having a fair is the civic equivalent of painting the living room puce, and any resultant cultural explosions like nylon or belly dancing are simply a by-product.

This is not to say that the cryptic carryings-on in Flushing Meadow will not do good to other people besides Mr. Robert Moses, who got us into this in the first place. The countries and corporations taking part are inevitably reassured about their own existence—"I have an exhibit at the Fair, therefore I am." A rosy glow also suffuses the consumer; no owner of a certain make of car is likely to view that alarming model of an automobile engine—the size of a small castle, sprayed in savage primary colors, and open to the public—without a wonderful sense of, somehow, *belonging*. It is sad to report that, seen from the far end of the car park, the New York World's Fair looks like a pickle factory severely damaged by blast; but close up many of the pavilions are quite handsome, and a few are downright beautiful. Some five hundred million dollars (or enough money to send a white mouse to Mars) have been spent, and eight thousand artisans kept out of mischief, on account of this disarming clutter of spheres, towers, chalets, temples, fountains, bells, aerial rides, H.M.S. *Bounty* (fake), Dead Sea Scrolls (real), folk dancers, waffles, steel bands, beer gardens, and electronic cavemen that grunt. (The rent of the site is probably the smallest single item; fifty cents a year for 646 acres is a bargain by anybody's standards.)

Seventy million people are expected to (heigh-ho) come to the Fair, and it has been calculated that if a visitor works at it five hours a day for a month he will have seen everything. He will have eaten remorselessly regional food in one hundred and fourteen different restaurants; watched American Indians smoke a salmon; heard a mechanical cow sing; gaped at Michelangelo's *Pietà*; found new hope for his declining years in the Pavilion of Dynamic Maturity; been spiritually got at by Billy Graham; and applauded the emergent nations of Burundi, Dahomey, Gabon, Togo, and the Malagasy Republic. He will also be, to put it politely, pooped; this Peace-Through-Understanding caper certainly takes it out of a chap.

No pains have been spared to make the exhibits as authentic as possible.

Closed-circuit TV beams the faces,
tear-stained or otherwise,
of mislaid children to points all around the Fair;
this is a help for parents who have
forgotten what the darlings look like.

Part of the Kodak exhibit is a model of the moon's surface, for people to take each other's pictures on. There will always be those who will settle for a trip to Cloud Nine.

ESPAÑA

Peace Through Understanding is a lovely thought,
and there is nothing like a glimpse of life as it is lived
in other lands for promoting international amity. Of course,
when it comes to Peace on Earth the system is apt to break down.

New York
WORLD'S FAIR
PEACE
through
UNDERSTANDING
VATICAN PAVILION
BILLY GRAHAM PAVILION
RUSSIAN ORTHODOX CHURCH
CHRISTIAN SCIENCE PAVILION
LATTER-DAY SAINTS
PROTESTANT CENTER
ORTHODOX CENTER
AVENUE OF
GARDEN OF MEDITATION
Billy Graham Pavilion
Sermon from Science
REPENT!
Ronald Searle

The General Motors exhibit,
which is entitled to call itself
a Futurama if that is what
it really wants, is the only building
shaped like a helicopter
that can accommodate seventy-two
thousand visitors a day.
It is unpredictable, self-willed,
and has the biggest tail fin in the world.

GM
General Motors

WISCONSIN
HERE IT IS –
THE LARGEST SINGLE
CHEESE EVER PRODUCED
New York
World's Fair

People are only human, which is why so many of us prefer animals.
The cheese in the Wisconsin Pavilion would,
if properly distributed, feed all the mice in Manhattan for a year.
Will no one undertake this eminently worthwhile project?

The Tower of Light gives off the strongest beam of light in the world. Twelve billion candle power tossed around in this irresponsible manner was bound to cause trouble.

As well as winetasting, the Paris Pavilion had a statue of Understanding Lifting the Veil of Prejudice. My God, these French!

TOWER OF LIGHT!

New York World's Fair
New York World's Fair
New York World's Fair
New York World's Fair

New York World's Fair
YORK FAIR

The Sinclair Refining Company
has generously provided a
child's garden of dinosaurs that
should help the kiddies to
wake up screaming for years to come.
And if an animated
fiber-glass dinosaur can't help
himself to a fifteen-foot
plastic orange, who can?

FLORIDA

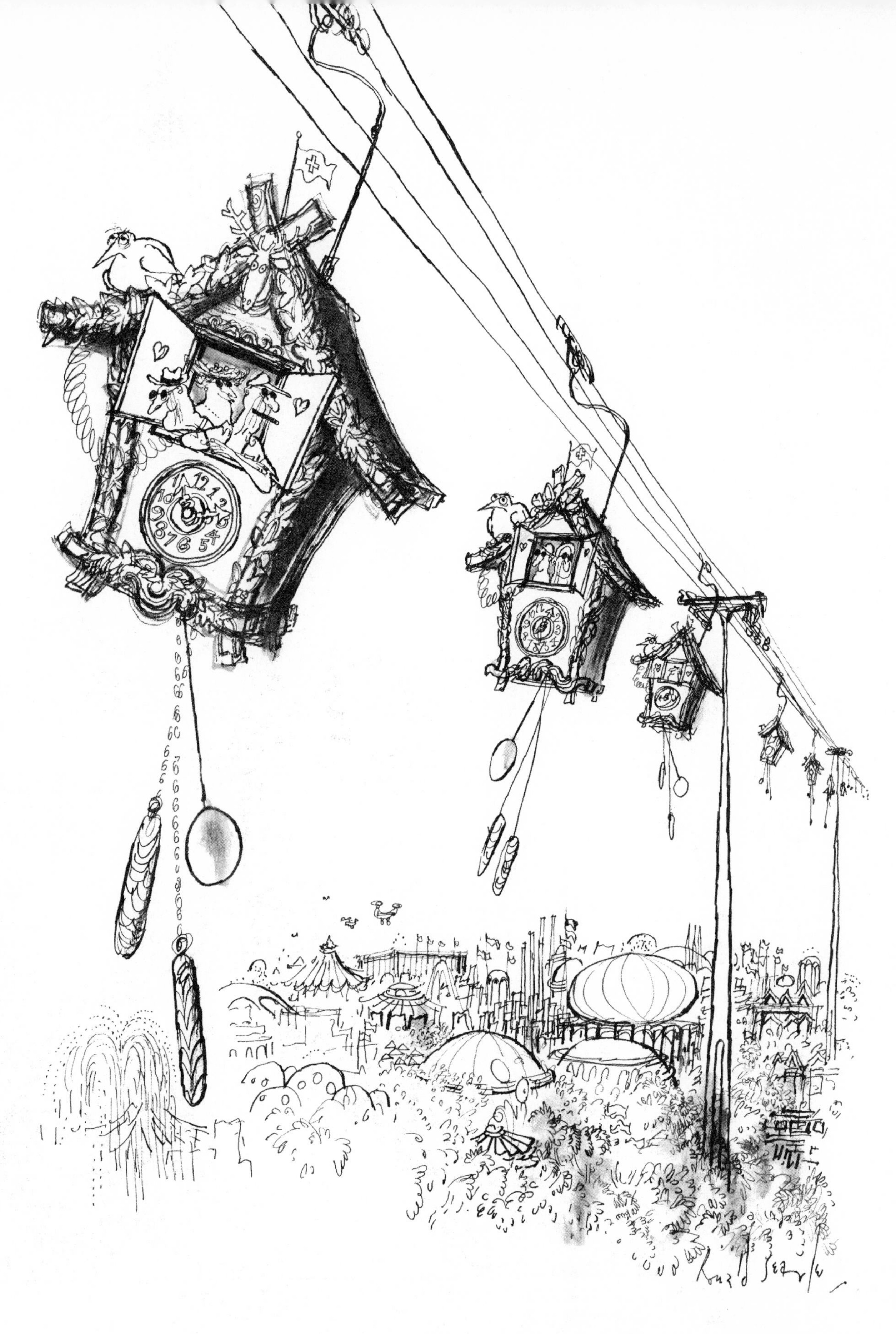

The Swiss Sky Ride lasts five minutes,
makes two complete circuits of the Fair,
and goes "Cuckoo" at the slightest provocation.

H
DEPARTMENT OF STATE
UNITED STATES OF AMERICA
Ronald Searle

Tourist Washington

Seven million sightseers come to Washington each year. (Probably many more set out but are permanently discouraged on arriving at the railroad station, of which the business end recalls a freight yard in Irkutsk at the low point of a Five Year Plan.) There is no truth in the rumor that six million of these visitors conspire to show up during a single weekend when the cherry blossom is out; it just seems that way.

Even without the cherry trees (a long-ago gift from the Japanese government, which was feeling friendly at the time) there is a lot to see: the Declaration of Independence, the sinister fingerprints preserved by the FBI, the Supreme Court in session, the Senate in genteel slumber, the Navaho gadgets in the aboriginal *boutique* run by the Department of the Interior, the Great Seal of the United States, the visiting potentates shaking down the State Department for a little loose change, the President's house, the first manned space capsule jauntily moored outside the Smithsonian, and the most beautiful Renoir in the world. Battered by culture, the tourist tends to collapse with a low moan on the steps of the Capitol. His brain is boggling, his shoes have shrunk a size and a half, and he has hardly begun; he hasn't been up the Washington Monument, he hasn't peeked into the Library of Congress, and he can't have himself photographed in front of the statue of Louis Daguerre because he doesn't know where it is. It is all *too much.*

Only it isn't, really. This beguiling, luminous, ungainly, fortuitously lovely and painfully important town is packed with Places of Interest, but there is no law that says you have to see the lot. If you would rather look at the view from the Capitol terrace than at the sculptures—many of them gouged by reverent hands from what appears to be cheese—in Statuary Hall, that is your business; while if you pass up the whole monument-and-masonry gamut in order to observe the dainty old-world rites of the House Un-American Activities Committee, you may learn more of what this curious place is about, or might be about if we are not careful, than on a dozen dutiful guided tours.

It's all there; take your pick. And after a thoughtful interlude with the marble likeness of Mr. Lincoln (which is larger than life only in the most technical sense), you might perhaps be moved to cross the river to Arlington Cemetery, where a small steady flame commemorates the man who also did the best he could in the time he was allowed.

The National Gallery of Art is made of pink marble, contains much of the free world's artistic heritage, and is a wonderful place to leave the children for the afternoon.

There are twelve million books and pamphlets in the Library of Congress,
with more of the stuff coming in like
bullets every day. Some people just don't seem to care.

DONT TOUCH
G
THE SMITHSONIAN
DIPLODOCUS . utah
Ronald Searle

The Smithsonian Institution, a Camelot-type confection
of towers, turrets, machicolations, and probably
oubliettes as well, is also a wonderful place
to leave the children; but sometimes the
little beasts will not leave well enough alone.

The White House has been through
a lot; it was burned by the British,
who were just passing through,
and tinkered with by President Truman.
Despite all this, it remains
a top tourist attraction.

Ronald Searle

No visit to Washington is complete without a tour of the FBI; besides, you meet such interesting people.

Sounding brass decorated with tinkling symbols patrols the Pentagon. We are not supposed to wonder what they are up to.

MILITARY INTELLIGENCE
2-A-870
JOINT CHIEFS OF STAFF
ADMITTANCE
BY
AUTHORISED
CREDENTIALS
ONLY
Ronald Searle
The Pentagon

The green stuff is always attractive, but American tourists suspect there must be a catch in it somewhere. Visitors from abroad know better.

THE UNITED STATES OF AMERICA
ONE DOLLAR
ONE DOLLAR
Ronald Searle

Ronald Searle

That fine body of men, the Washington corps of sherpas, has done noble work over the years. Everest was a breeze compared with the steps of the Capitol.

It's not so much the aprons, it's the risk of losing
a finger that haunts the novice Mason.

Tribal America

That fragrant legend, the Average American—you know the fellow, he's the one with the fractional children, the man you never meet—is many things: he is loyal, brave, reverent, light beige in color, and in winter probably wears two-thirds of a hat. But above all he is a joiner. (He always was; even de Tocqueville noticed it.)

Out of a population of a hundred and eighty million, roughly a hundred million belong to *something*. It may be vaguely philanthropic, like the Lions or the Elks; rigidly ethnic, like the Ancient Order of Hibernians; frankly dotty, like the Society for the Prevention of Calling Sleeping Car Porters George; or even genealogical like the Society of the Cincinatti or the Daughters of the American Revolution. (These corporate romps are only sporadically co-ed; besides the female auxiliaries of male totems, the girls have their own outfits, many of them devoted to upstaging each other about whose ancestors came over on which boat.)

The declared objects of the various associations may be as diverse as the return of Prohibition, the advancement of nudism, and the preservation of barber-shop-quartet singing in America—and those who have never tried to cross a hotel lobby jammed with dedicated Preservers all singing "Sweet Adeline" can have no conception, simply no conception at all, of what togetherness really means. But the strongest reason is common to all, and seldom publicized. On gray mornings when the wind is in the northeast and the plumbing is on the blink and there is nothing in the mail but bills and soap coupons, a hundred and eighty million other Americans can seem to be too many. But convert a portion of that incalculable crowd into fellow Rotarians, fellow Shriners, or even—it's no good sweeping the embarrassing ones under that old white sheet—even fellow members of the Ku Klux Klan, and suddenly the world is full of buddies.

The whole population is rather too large for comfort; the family is rather too small; poised cozily in between is the club, the league, the society, the dear welcoming wigwam of the Improved Order of Red Men. Liberty and equality we're still working on, but when it comes to fraternity America stands alone.

The Barbershop Quartet will probably outlast the barber.

An Elk about to lock antlers.

A Shriner in full cry.

One of the Peewit Patrol's stanchest,
and indeed oldest, members.

The Daughters of the American Revolution
march boldly backward to victory.

KEEP RIGHT
Ronald Searle

Ronald Searle
Miami Beach

Florida

There is no such place as Florida. It is hard to say where Ronald Searle was all those weeks (Oz, perhaps?) because he forgot to write; but it can't have been Florida, as there is no such place. Psychiatrists who have made a study of the problem say that the Florida syndrome—which comprises the double delusion that Florida exists and that one has been there—is of some antiquity. The first recorded sufferer was Ponce de León, who maintained to his dying day that he had discovered the area in 1513; he also said that he had found there the Fountain of Youth, the waters of which contained the elixir of eternal life, and as things turned out there wasn't a word of truth in that either. After Ponce de León there was Hernando de Soto, who subsequently came to his senses and discovered the Mississippi River, which *does* exist; but by that time the damage was done.

In 1819 the United States government formally purchased Florida from the Spaniards, who galloped all the way to the bank in case somebody should find out the truth before the check was cleared. It was another hundred years, however, before the Florida syndrome reached the status of mass delusion, with thousands of giddy investors who had never been farther south than Battery Park paying a thousand dollars each for building lots which were, by and large, under water.

There are plenty of people like this still about. Put to them the proposition that Florida is simply not there, and they will make the most heartrending efforts to preserve the cherished error. Such dreamers have been known to claim that Miami Beach at least has to be real, since Al Capone used to live there. There is nothing to be gained by bandying words with the sort of person who thinks that a man who lied about his income tax would tell the truth about anything else; but just consider what, if we believe in Florida, we are required to believe in along with it. Cocoa Beach, where they take the Man in the Moon seriously; alligator farms; Miami; Weekiwachee Springs, which claims to have mermaids; and a big swamp called the Everglades where there are strangler figs. Do you believe in strangler figs?

Well that clears that up. Only one tiny nagging doubt remains: since we are agreed that there is no such place as Florida, where the hell do all those oranges come from?

Sarasota became a tent away from tent for circus people in 1929, when John Ringling made it the winter quarters of his motley troupe. Sand makes a change from tanbark between the toes.

St. Petersburg, the Retirement Capital of the United States, has thirty-eight hundred sidewalk benches. At peak capacity of six senior citizens to a bench, this means that about twenty thousand people can sit down at the same time. Most of them do.

Some people will do anything for a free handout;
this is the sort of thing that keeps the staff at
Marineland constantly on the qui vive.

There are two species of alligator in the world;
the other one is found in China,
where farming tends to be collective.

Florida

Marine romps of every kind are commonplace along
Florida's eighty-five hundred miles of coastline.
As if this were not enough, there are thirty thousand
lakes for boating, swimming, and the pursuit of mermaids.

Florida's coastal waters bulge with marlin, tuna,
and other sizable prizes. Unlike so many rewarding
activities, saltwater sport fishing needs no license.

FL 9186B
TUNA

Fort Lauderdale is where
the boys are. Sometimes the parents
are there too, hiding from their
effervescent young
inside portable shelters—
a habit shared by some of
the simpler orders of creation.

Northern resorts have
summer people; Palm Beach
has winter people, and most of them
are filthy with the stuff.
They are known for conservatism,
exigency, and the eerie palaces
in which they live—
a Disney dream of old Castile.

Sanibel Island, off Fort Myers,
is world-famous for its shells,
which include such exotics
as the lion's paw,
the angel's wing, and the
Chinese alphabet. Less widely known
is the Love Goddess of Shaker Heights;
but clearly there is something
for everyone on Sanibel.

Only Florida could make an asset out of a mangrove swamp.
The Everglades are the home of the gumbo limbo (a kind of tree),
the roseate spoonbill, and other things as well.

Four hundred and fifty years after Ponce de León,
the fountain of youth flows on in St. Augustine; eighty cents
admission seems a small price for perpetual springtime.

Science makes life easier for us all;
at Cocoa Beach the countdown has been
superseded by simplified methods.

1/27/65